D1707923

DOMINICAN REPUBLIC

By Donna Reynolds and
Laura L. Sullivan

EXPLORING
WORLD
CULTURES

Cavendish
Square

Published in 2023 by Cavendish Square Publishing, LLC
2544 Clinton Street, Buffalo, NY 14224

Website: cavendishsq.com

This publication represents the opinions and views of the author based on their personal experience, knowledge, and research. The information in this book serves as a general guide only. The author and publisher have used their best efforts in preparing this book and disclaim liability rising directly or indirectly from the use and application of this book.

All websites were available and accurate when this book was sent to press.

Library of Congress Cataloging-in-Publication Data

Names: Reynolds, Donna, author. | Sullivan, Laura L., 1974- author.
Title: Dominican Republic / Donna Reynolds; Laura L. Sullivan.
Description: New York, NY: Cavendish Square Publishing, 2023. | Series:
    Exploring world cultures | Includes index.
Identifiers: LCCN 2022023847 | ISBN 9781502667175 (library binding) | ISBN
    9781502667168 (paperback) | ISBN 9781502667182 (ebook)
Subjects: LCSH: Dominican Republic--Juvenile literature.
Classification: LCC F1934.2 .R49 2023 | DDC 972.93--dc23/eng/20220520
LC record available at https://lccn.loc.gov/2022023847

Writers: Laura L Sullivan; Donna Reynolds (second edition)
Editor: Jennifer Lombardo
Copyeditor: Shannon Harts
Designer: Andrea Davison-Bartolotta

The photographs in this book are used by permission and through the courtesy of: Cover kate_sept2004/iStockphoto.com; p. 4 Dianna Tatkow/Shutterstock.com; p. 5 Seth Michael/Shutterstock.com; p. 6 dreii/Shutterstock.com; p. 7 Rainer Lesniewski/Shutterstock.com; p. 8 John Mitchell/Alamy Stock Photo; p. 9 State Department photo by Ron Przysucha/Public Domain; p. 10 Felix Lipov/Shutterstock.com; p. 11 gt29/Shutterstock.com; pp. 13 (top), 23, 25 Matyas Rehak/Shutterstock.com; p. 13 (bottom) photopixel/Shutterstock.com; p. 14 Edwin Godinho/Shutterstock.com; p. 15 Jenya_TarasoF/Shutterstock.com; p. 16 ADOLFO SESTO/Shutterstock.com; p. 17 Wirestock Creators/Shutterstock.com; p. 18 ooo.photography/Shutterstock.com; p. 19 Aleksandr Rybalko/Shutterstock.com; p. 20 Viveronelle/Shutterstock.com; p. 21 David Antonio Lopez Moya/Shutterstock.com; p. 22 Alexandre Laprise/Shutterstock.com; pp. 24, 29 Mario De Moya F/Shutterstock.com; p. 26 Martin Corr/Shutterstock.com; p. 27 Keeton Gale/Shutterstock.com; p. 28 Charles Pena/Shutterstock.com.

Some of the images in this book illustrate individuals who are models. The depictions do not imply actual situations or events.

CPSIA compliance information: Batch #CW23CSQ: For further information contact Cavendish Square Publishing LLC at 1-877-980-4450.

Printed in the United States of America

Find us on

CONTENTS

INTRODUCTION

People have lived in what's now known as the Dominican Republic for about 2,000 years. However, when Christopher Columbus arrived in the country, life for the Native people changed completely. Today, the **culture** in the Dominican Republic is a mix of old Native ways and newer European practices.

The Dominican Republic has rain forests and caves in addition to its famous beaches.

Visitors are welcomed in this country. Dominicans are known as friendly people who love dancing, music, and art. Some styles of art are **unique** to the country. For example, merengue is a style of both music and dance that was created in the Dominican Republic.

There are a lot of great things about the Dominican Republic. However, like all countries, it has its problems too. Parts of the country are very poor, and women are not always treated equally to men. However, Dominicans love their country and want it to be the best it can be, so they work hard to fix its problems.

Many Dominicans are poor even though the amount of money the country has is growing.

GEOGRAPHY

The island that the countries of the Dominican Republic and Haiti share is called Hispaniola. The Dominican Republic takes up the eastern two-thirds of the island. It has an **area** of about 18,704 square miles (48,442 square kilometers). Haiti covers the western third of the island.

FACT!

Hispaniola is the second-largest island in the Caribbean.

Larimar is found on Hispaniola.

This map shows how Hispaniola is separated.

The Dominican Republic has four main mountain ranges, four major rivers, and wide valleys. It is best known for its beaches along the coast of the beautiful Caribbean Sea.

In general, the country is very warm, especially the coast. **Tropical** storms called hurricanes sometimes strike the island. The Dominican Republic has the highest mountains in the Caribbean, and the air in those mountains is the coolest in the entire Caribbean.

A RARE STONE

Pectolite is a common whitish-gray crystal, but it has a blue form too. Blue pectolite, called larimar, is found only in the Dominican Republic.

7

HISTORY

The Native people of Hispaniola are called the Taíno. They have lived there for at least 2,000 years. In 1492, Christopher Columbus landed on Hispaniola and claimed it for Spain. Columbus and the Taíno fought. He enslaved the people, and many died from diseases such as smallpox.

These rock carvings are believed to have been made by the Taíno people.

NOT REALLY GONE

For years, people thought Columbus had killed all the Taíno. Today, we know the Spanish just started pretending they didn't exist anymore.

The Dominican Republic was controlled by other countries—including Spain, France, and Haiti—until it became independent for good in 1844. Between 1844 and 1982, the Dominican Republic was ruled mainly by **dictators** who told the people what to do. They hurt a lot of people, and some made the country worse by making bad decisions and spending too much money. Today, the Dominican Republic's leaders aren't dictators, and the people aren't hurt the way they were in the past.

FACT!

Santo Domingo, the capital of the Dominican Republic, is the oldest European settlement in the western part of the world.

Luis Abinader was elected president in 2020.

GOVERNMENT

The Dominican Republic is a democracy. This means the people who live there vote on who gets to hold positions in the government. The country has three branches of government: executive, legislative, and judicial. The executive branch **enforces** the laws. It is headed by the president, who is also in charge of the military. There is a vote for president and vice president every four years.

FACT!
The president chooses a governor for every **province** in the Dominican Republic.

The president lives in the National Palace.

The legislative branch makes the laws people have to follow. The Dominican Republic's legislative branch includes a Senate and a Chamber of Deputies. These members are also elected.

The judicial branch, which includes the Supreme Court, decides what the laws mean and what should happen to people who don't follow them.

A RECENT DOCUMENT

The country has had many **constitutions**. The one it uses today went into effect in 2015.

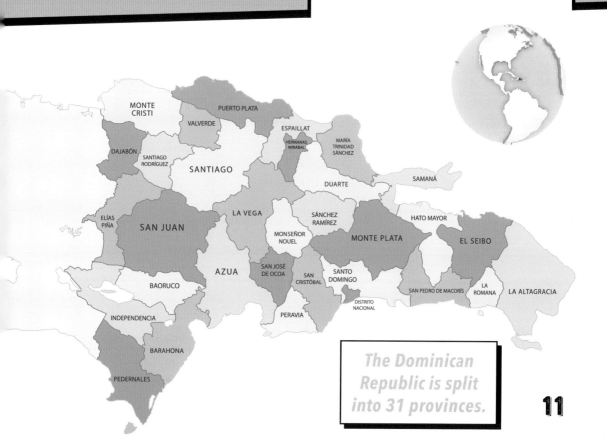

The Dominican Republic is split into 31 provinces.

THE ECONOMY

There are a lot of different parts to the Dominican Republic's economy, or the way goods and services are made and sold in a country. The biggest one is tourism. Visitors who stay in hotels, buy food, and shop add a lot of money to the economy. Mining and farming also bring money to the country because they give the government things to sell to other countries.

Even though the economy is doing well, many Dominicans still don't have enough money. The government doesn't always take care of its people, and natural **disasters** such as hurricanes often destroy people's property. Not everyone has clean water or working electricity in their homes. On farms, some young children work instead of going to school. This makes it hard to find jobs later.

REMITTANCES

Dominicans living in other countries send money home to help their family. This is called sending remittances. It's a big part of the country's economy.

Farming makes up about 11 percent of the country's economy.

Hurricanes, floods, and other natural disasters are a problem in the Dominican Republic.

THE ENVIRONMENT

The Dominican Republic has many different kinds of plants and animals in its environment, or natural surroundings. These include coral reefs, iguanas, frogs, and several kinds of **endangered** birds. However, this wildlife is in trouble because of human activities. For example, many tourists who come to the country don't clean up after themselves. This means there's a lot of trash on the Dominican Republic's beaches that can hurt animals.

FACT!
An endangered bird called the Ridgway's hawk is found only in the Dominican Republic.

The palmchat is the country's national bird.

In the mountains, people cut down trees to sell the wood, plant crops, and raise livestock. People have been cutting down too many trees, which is bad for the animals and other plants that use those trees for homes and food. Dominicans are working on planting trees and cutting down fewer of them each year.

HELPING THE HUMPBACKS

Every year between December and March, humpback whales gather in the Silver Bank near the Dominican Republic to give birth. This area has been named a **sanctuary** to keep the whales safe.

Whale-watching tours are popular in the Dominican Republic.

15

THE PEOPLE TODAY

Most of the 11 million people who live in the Dominican Republic are multiracial. That means they have **ancestors** who came from both Europe and Africa. About 16 percent of the population is white, and 11 percent is Black. We don't know exactly how many people are Taíno because the government still does not count them.

Dominicans are proud of their country and work to make it better.

Santo Domingo is the capital of the Dominican Republic.

There are also many immigrants, or people who have moved from another country, in the Dominican Republic. Many come from other Caribbean nations. Some come from places such as China, Japan, and Arab nations. They make up about 1 percent of the total number of people living in the country.

FINDING THE TAÍNO

Many people have known they're Taíno for hundreds of years. In 2018, scientists found **DNA** that proved it to the rest of the world.

Most of the population lives in cities. More than 3 million people live in Santo Domingo alone.

17

LIFESTYLE

Family is very important to Dominicans. A person's grandparents, parents, and children may all live in the same house or neighborhood. Family members take care of each other and treat each other with respect. Dominicans are also known for being friendly and outgoing. They make friends easily and are very welcoming to guests.

FACT!
Dominicans highly value **loyalty** and trust.

A Dominican family is shown here.

18

By law, Dominican women are equal to men in all ways. However, that is not always true in life. Women are sometimes expected to stay at home and take care of their families instead of working. Violence, or harm, against women as well as immigrants is a problem in many parts of the Dominican Republic. Several groups are working to change this.

TAKING THEIR TIME

Unlike in many cities in the United States, people usually don't rush in the Dominican Republic. It's normal for parties and meetings to start late.

Dominicans are often friendly to strangers.

RELIGION

The Dominican Republic gives its people freedom of religion, or faith. This means anyone living there can practice any religion or no religion at all. About 49 percent are Catholic, 26 percent are Protestant, and 21 percent follow no religion. There are also a small number of people practicing other religions, including Buddhists, Muslims, and Jews.

These Dominican girls are in a Catholic church.

Some people practice a type of religion called Vudú. Many who follow this religion combine African beliefs with Christianity. However, Vudú is not as common in the Dominican Republic as a similar religion, Vodou, is in Haiti. Vudú is often looked down upon by white Europeans, so people who practice it have kept it mostly secret over the years.

FACT!

Most countries in the world, including the Dominican Republic, are becoming less religious.

THE OLDEST CATHEDRAL

A cathedral is an important kind of Christian church. The oldest cathedral in the Americas is the Cathedral of Santa María la Menor in the Dominican Republic.

Shown here is the Cathedral of Santa María la Menor.

LANGUAGE

The official language of the Dominican Republic is Spanish. However, it isn't quite the same as the Spanish that is spoken in Spain. Dominican Spanish is a mix of old Taíno words and Spanish words. Some of the Spanish words are so old they are no longer spoken in Spain. At school, children are taught in Spanish. Schools also teach English and French.

FACT!
The Taíno language is now extinct. This means no one still speaks it.

The law says all Dominican children have to go to school.

Another language spoken in the country is Haitian Creole. It is spoken by Haitians living in the Dominican Republic. Haitian Creole combines words from Spanish, French, and West African countries. About 12,000 people also speak Samaná English. This form of English was first spoken by Black people who moved to the Dominican Republic in the 1820s. Chinese is also becoming popular because there are many Chinese immigrants living in the country.

Shown here is Chinatown in Santo Domingo.

EXCHANGING WORDS

One Taíno word that made its way into both Spanish and English is barbacoa, which means barbecue.

ARTS AND FESTIVALS

Merengue is a style of music that was created in the Dominican Republic and later became popular in other Latin American countries, especially Puerto Rico. It combines African and Spanish music styles.

WRITING IS AN ART

There are many famous Dominican authors, including Junot Díaz, Julia Alvarez, Angie Cruz, and Elizabeth Acevedo. Many write about what it's like to be Dominican.

Guloya dancers wear colorful costumes that include masks.

The Dominican Republic has festivals, or special gatherings, all year round. The biggest are the carnivals held in February. Music, dancing, and parades are common. Dance is a big part of many festivals, such as the Merengue Festival in July. The Guloya Festival in January celebrates guloya, a style of **theatrical** dance that's unique to the Dominican Republic.

The country has also produced many artists. A popular style of art is folk art. It is painted with many bright colors. Art is an important part of Dominican culture.

FACT!
Merengue is also a style of dance.

These three instruments are needed to play merengue.

FUN AND PLAY

Because of the Dominican Republic's warm weather and beautiful natural environment, many Dominicans like to spend time outside. Just like the tourists who visit, residents often go to the beach or enjoy scuba diving or snorkeling. Fishing, surfing, and boating are also popular with many Dominicans.

Many Dominicans enjoy going to the beach.

EL PAÑUELO (THE HANDKERCHIEF)

This popular Dominican kids' game involves two teams that try to steal a handkerchief and bring it back to their base without being tagged by the other team.

Baseball is the most popular sport in the Dominican Republic. Children often learn to play at a young age. Adults support the country's baseball league, which has six teams. Manny Ramirez, Albert Pujols, and David Ortiz are some famous Dominican Major League Baseball (MLB) players.

Boxing is another popular sport. Many world champion boxers come from the Dominican Republic. The country has also taken part in the Olympics since 1964. In 1984, boxer Pedro Julio Nolasco won the Dominican Republic's first Olympic medal.

Albert Pujols is a popular MLB player.

FOOD

Like every country, food is a big part of Dominican culture. Some dishes served here are popular all over Latin America. Others are found only in the Dominican Republic. Many Dominican dishes come from Spanish culture, from Africa, and from meals the Taíno make.

A FRUITFUL COUNTRY

Many fruits grow in the Dominican Republic, including pineapple, guava, papaya, watermelon, passion fruit, and mango.

Shown here is a popular Dominican breakfast.

28

Most meals include some kind of meat. In fact, a stew called *sancocho* includes seven different kinds of meat. Pork is a favorite throughout the country, and seafood is eaten near the coast. A common breakfast is fried eggs, fried salami, fried cheese, and *mangú*—a uniquely Dominican food made of mashed green plantains. Lunch is usually the biggest meal of the day. Rice, beans, and some kind of meat are often served. Dinner is usually lighter. One of the country's most popular desserts is a cake with pineapple filling.

FACT!
Other countries have their own recipes for sancocho.

Another uniquely Dominican dessert is habichuelas con dulce (sweet cream of beans).

GLOSSARY

ancestor: A relative who lived long before you.

area: The amount of surface included within limits.

constitution: A document that describes the laws of a country.

culture: The beliefs and ways of life of a certain group of people.

dictator: Someone who rules a country by force.

disaster: An event that causes much suffering or loss.

DNA: Part of the body that carries genetic information, which gives the instructions for life.

endangered: In danger of dying out.

enforce: To make sure people obey the law.

loyalty: Being true and constant in support of someone or something.

province: An area of a country.

sanctuary: A place that provides safety or protection.

theatrical: For or relating to the presentation of plays.

tropical: Having to do with the warm parts of Earth near the equator.

unique: Out of the ordinary, or the only one of its kind.

FIND OUT MORE

Books

Gottschall, Meghan. *Hola, Dominican Republic*. Ann Arbor, MI: Cherry Lake Publishing, 2021.

Rechner, Amy. *The Dominican Republic*. Minnetonka, MN: Bellwether Media, 2020.

Website

Ducksters: Dominican Republic
www.ducksters.com/geography/country.php?country=Dominican%20Republic
Learn more facts about the Dominican Republic.

Video

YouTube: "Puerto Rican and Dominican Dance—Merengue"
www.youtube.com/watch?v=lcPHaV3p6S4
Watch a kids' dance group dance the merengue to merengue music.

INDEX